THE GREEK MUSEUMS

Herakleion Museum
AND ARCHAEOLOGICAL SITES OF CRETE

Athens 1977

Publishers: George A. Christopoulos, John C. Bastias
Translation: Robert Lidell
Art Director: Chrysé Daskalopoulou
Special Photography: Makis Skiadaresis, Spyros Tsavdaroglou and Nikos Kontos
Colour separation: Pietro Carlotti

THE GREEK MUSEUMS

Herakleion Museum
AND ARCHAEOLOGICAL SITES OF CRETE

MANOLIS ANDRONICOS

Professor of Archaeology at the University of Thessalonike

EKDOTIKE ATHENON S.A.
Athens 1977

MINOAN CRETE
AND THE HERAKLEION MUSEUM

A BRIEF HISTORY OF THE MUSEUM

The Museum of Herakleion contains a unique collection of Cretan antiquities. The very ancient civilization of Crete had remained practically unknown to research until the closing years of the last century. When large-scale archaeological excavations were undertaken, the magnificent relics that had lain buried for centuries in the soil of the island, were brought to light and preserved in their place of origin. Today, very few examples of the Minoan civilization are to be seen in the Museums of Europe and America, and all the treasures of the ancient history of Crete, which constitutes the first brilliant chapter in Greek history, have found a permanent home in the Museum of Herakleion. In this part of the Hellenic world there appeared for the first time a great civilization with outstanding artistic manifestations, admirable social and state organization, and unprecedented economic development. Sole witness to these achievements are the carefully arranged and finely displayed archaeological finds in the Museum of Herakleion.

It should be noted that the archaeologist responsible for the display of material in the Museum, Professor N. Platon, a distinguished scholar in Cretan civilization, was fortunate in having at his disposal a new building with a rationally planned layout, specially designed for the antiquities it was to house. Professor Platon made the most of this opportunity. Later, in 1964, when a new wing of four galleries was added to the Museum, the present Curator, Dr. St. Alexiou, completed the exhibition in the same exemplary and scholarly fashion.

At this point we should also mention the names of J. Hazzidakis and St. Xanthoudidis, the pioneer Cretan archaeologists who founded both the first Museum (1904 - 1912) and the Greek Archaeological Service in Crete. Possibly attracted by the early finds of the Herakleiot antiquarian Minos Kalokairinos, who discovered the palace of Knossos in 1878 and attempted the earliest excavations on the site, J. Hazzidakis, then president of the local "Society for the Promotion of Education", started a collection of antiquities as early as 1883, long before Sir Arthur Evans began his great excavations in 1900. This Society, in collaboration with Professor F. Halbherr, excavated the well-known cave sites *Idaion Antron* on Mt. Ida and *Speos Eileithyias* at Amnisos (fig. 16), which yielded a great number of valuable votive offerings. The famous inscription of the laws of Gortyn, perhaps the most important epigraphic text of ancient Greece, was unearthed in that same year.

HISTORIC INTRODUCTION: Chronological division of the Minoan civilization

In the Museum of Herakleion the visitor may enjoy and the scholar may study all the relics of Minoan civilization, with the exception, of course, of the most significant antiquities — the buildings themselves. A tour of the ruins so far uncovered by excavations is recommended before a visit to the Museum, as it will afford a better understanding of the splendid features of the Cretan world. Architecture is the highest and most complex expression of the character of every civilization, since it reflects its economic activity, political power, religious faith and artistic inspiration. In Crete, moreover, the culminating phase of the Minoan civilization (1700 - 1450 B.C.) was founded on the great palace centres: the magnificent palaces had been the cradle of every creation and activity which spread over the entire island, or at least over its central and eastern parts. The building of palaces seems to have marked both the cultural and political history of Minoan Crete most profoundly. The recently applied division of the Minoan civilization into three phases — The Pre-Palace period (2700 1900 B.C.), the Old Palace period (1900 - 1700 B.C.) and the New Palace period (1700 - 1450 B.C.) — is not a mere archaeological convention, but indicates actual divisions in that civilization.

Neolithic and Pre-Palace period

The earliest finds recovered from various Cretan sites have been assigned to the Neolithic period. However, the so-called Minoan civilization emerged with such intensity in the period following the Neolithic, that the earliest investigators regarded it as a "sudden miracle" and attributed it to the invasion of a new people from Asia Minor. We have now reached the conclusion that the change effected was partly due to the infiltration of these tribes, but that it was neither sudden nor ignorant of the achievements of the earlier Neolithic inhabitants, who had survived the invasion and welcomed the great discovery, i.e. bronze, which the invaders brought with them. Thus the beginnings of the great era of Cretan history are to be traced to this Pre-Palace period, when the inhabitants of settlements scattered throughout the island, and chiefly the central and eastern sections, initiated a rapid development of the arts and crafts. It is worth noticing that this early period produced fine examples of all the branches of art, which were to reach their height in the following periods: principally pottery, but also metal-work, gold-work, stone-carving, and particularly seal-engraving. The objects exhibited in the galleries of the Museum of Herakleion demonstrate with unbroken continuity the achievements of the Minoans in every field. Notwithstanding the remarkable development of Crete during this early phase, the island retained the character of a society based primarily on a fragmentary agricultural economy, and, to a lesser degree, on trade and some sort of industry. We must assume that this fragmentation also existed in public life, which cannot possibly have achieved advanced political systems, capable of leading to the creation of a strong state power.

Old Palace period

Archaeological finds, which mark the beginning of the Old Palace period, testify to the vital change that was to lead to a new social and political organization. In about 1900 B.C. palaces were built for the first time at key positions: at Knossos, Phaistos, Malia, and perhaps at two or three other places (Hania?). This indicates the concentration of authority in the hands of strong leaders, able to rule over large areas and exercise control over trade and all produce, agricultural and industrial. The parallel development of the palace centres also signifies their peaceful coexistence and the absence of warlike antagonism. The contemporaneous creation of large towns bears witness to the social change that had taken place in these years, while the strongly religious character of many of the finds leads us to believe that the whole system had the same theocratic character as that encountered in other great Eastern nations, such as Egypt and Assyria. It is therefore not surprising that at this age the Cretans should discover and use the art of writing in its most ancient form, the hieroglyphic; it is also natural that there should be a rapid development in all the branches of art which had already borne fine fruit in the previous period.

New Palace period

Archaeologists have succeeded in proving that these "old" palaces were destroyed three times in the two hundred years of their existence. But while the two first destructions were not total, the third, which took place c. 1700 B.C., and seems to have been caused by an earthquake, had terrible results. It is however strange that the ruin of the palaces was not followed by a more general collapse of political activity. On the contrary, life on the island continued to flourish, and the New Palace period that follows (1700-1450 B.C.) is the most productive and creative phase of Minoan civilization. New palaces were raised on the site of the old, after the area had been levelled; and other palaces, such as that of Zakros, or rich villas were speedily built, and in considerable numbers. Everything testifies to the fact that the ancient tradition which elevated King Minos to the sphere of myth, and preserved the memory of his sea-power and his justice, was not a figment of fantasy. The excavations of Sir Arthur Evans at Knossos were needed before we could understand the myth of the labyrinth, or realize that even if Daidalos is a mythical name, his achievements were not mythical.

PALACES, VILLAS AND URBAN CENTRES

The architecture of the new palaces presents all the elements illustrative of Minoan society and civilization. The largest palace, that of Knossos, invites the visitor to complete it with his imagination. Round the vast central court rise many-storeyed buildings; open corridors, numerous staircases, and walls pierced with many doors, lofty light-wells, coloured surfaces and columns, and frescoes brightly coloured, form a whole where the masses lose their weight and seem to move in light and shade affording protection from the warm climate of this Mediterranean island and offering a visible picture of the active and cheerful world that lived in buildings like these.

The palace of Knossos, like the other palaces of Minoan Crete, was not only the political, but also the religious and economic centre of the entire region (fig. 1). All around it stretched a populous city (Evans estimated the inhabitants to about 80,000), and at a small distance there was the harbour, sheltering the mighty fleet of the sea-ruling power.

The 22,000 square metres of the palace area included innumerable rooms and quarters suited to the diverse needs and functions of royal power. The east wing, consisting of four or five stories, was the residence of the royal family; the king's quarters were larger and more opulent, the queen's smaller but more elegant. The most imposing room, containing the throne which has survived intact, was on the ground floor of the west section of the palace (fig. 5); it was reached from the north entrance, where the road from the harbour came to an end (fig. 2). Next to the throne-room there were various compartments reserved for religious functions, such as the tripartive sanctuary (fig. 4), the sacred crypts, the treasuries, the lustration basins; the vicinity of these installations indicate that the throne-room was the seat of the Priest-King, the absolute ruler who embodied the god himself. However, political power was founded upon a strong economic basis resulting from a highly developed home industry and intensive trade. It is practically certain that these economic activities were under the King's control, as evidenced by the numerous palace store-rooms containing enormous pithoi (fig. 3), and, above all, by the various workshops (stone-cutting, pottery, seal-engraving etc.) clustered around the north-east wing of the palace.

The second most important palace of Crete was that of Phaistos, on the south coast of the island (figs. 6-7). Smaller than the palace of Knossos (about 9,000 square metres), it has retained all the basic features characteristic of Minoan palaces. Here again, the installations reserved for religious functions are located in the west wing, whereas the royal quarters are at the end of the north wing, with a magnificent view of the mountain range of Ida. The workshops are on the west side of the palace; the most interesting among them is a bronze-smelting kiln. From the architectural point of view, this palace is better organized; there is a consistence about the arrangement of the rooms which is due to the fact that they were built according to a single plan. Whereas the palace of Knossos underwent a series of alterations and additions, the palace of Phaistos was built from the beginning according to a fresh plan, after the destruction of the old palace in an earthquake. Even the building material used at Phaistos was of better quality, while architectural details show greater skill and care. Archaeologists believe that the large royal villa (at a distance of 3 kms. from Phaistos) on the hill of Hagia Triada surrounded by the green valley of Geropotamos, probably served as a summer residence of the king who reigned in the great palace of southern Crete (figs. 13-14).

The third important palace in Crete is at Malia, at a relatively small distance east of Knossos (figs. 8-10). Although it is as large as the Phaistos palace, neither its architecture nor the building material that went into it, nor its interior decoration can be compared to those of the two palaces mentioned previously. However, excavations in this area have yielded some important results; several housing-blocks were discovered around the palace, with well-designed roads and with buildings that have enabled the excavators to assume the existence of an *Agora* and a *Prytaneion*. If the assumption is finally proved correct, it should imply that the seeds of what was to become the Greek *polis* (city-state) in historical times, were to be found at a very early date in the remote world of Cretan prehistory.

The last palace, unearthed by the recent excavations of Professor N. Platon, is at Zakros (fig. 11), on the east coast of Crete, exactly opposite the coasts of Syria and Phoenicia, situated at a point of extreme importance for the trade activities of that period. It is smaller than the other Cretan palaces, but presents the same basic structure and confirms all the conclusions to be drawn from the larger palaces of central Crete. Moreover, Zakros was the first to yield treasures that have survived intact, for its final destruction occurred so suddenly, it seems, that its residents did not have time to salvage anything, as indicated by details such as remnants of food and cooking utensils found in place.

Remains of various villas and farm-houses help us to complete the picture of Minoan architecture and life as it was lived on that prosperous island in prehistoric times; for example, there are the ruins at Tylissos (fig. 12), Vathypetro (fig. 15) and Amnisos (fig. 17), and even the humbler, yet by no means less interesting finds from smaller settlements, like that of Gournia. The visitor who wishes to form a correct idea of the Minoan world can and should first study these regions and wander among the age-old ruins of these brilliant specimens of a wise Mediterranean architecture.

THE MUSEUM — VASES

After a tour of the sites, a visit to the Museum of Herakleion, where all the finds of the Cretan excavations are housed, provides further knowledge of this civilization, its art and way of life. In the Museum galleries, therefore, one can follow the history of Minoan art in all its branches: pottery, first and foremost, then stone-carving, seal-engraving, metal-work, work in gold, and finally the great painting of the frescoes.

Pottery and vase-painting

Pottery was among the first arts of Neolithic man, and the earliest examples found in Crete are assigned to that age. But the first rich collections of vases displayed in the Museum belong to the Proto-Minoan or Pre-Palace period (2700-1900 B.C.). Already by this time the Cretan craftsmen knew the use of the potter's wheel and were thus able to give elegant and elaborate shapes to their pottery. The cases of the Museum contain a delightful large collection of ware from Eastern Crete, in the style called Vasiliki, from the site where the greatest number and the most typical examples were found: jugs with a high beak-shaped spout, and above all broad open vases with vertical handle and spout like the beak of an exotic bird. Their dark surface is brightened by a rich light-coloured decoration in which the curved line dominates, often in its most dynamic shape, the spiral. In the most evolved examples of this pottery the decoration has already achieved a polychromy, which is in keeping with its rich foliate patterns.

The Kamares Ware

This charming polychrome decoration is again encountered in the finest examples of Minoan pottery which represent almost the entire Old Palace period (1900-1700 B.C.) and owe their name, Kamares Ware, to the cave where they were first discovered (figs. 19 and 21). Their technical perfection is on a level with their high artistic value. The vibrant colours, the incredible variety of decorative themes with their flexible and spontaneous spreading over the surface of the vase, suggest that the society which created and used this ware must have lived an easy, festal, mediterranean life, rejoicing in the sunlight and worshipping nature. Yet, the decoration of the Kamares Ware does not include naturalistic forms. The golden, blue, yellow, red lines and surfaces, with their forceful and elastic curves, spread over the vase, following its shape and emphasizing the characteristic features of its structure. If the complexity of these curves should give the visitor the impression of an exotic picture and bring strange plants and animals to his mind, he should not allow himself to be deceived into thinking that this was part of the artist's intention. However, in the process of creation, the artist was beginning to distinguish some forms that were to develop later into well-known plant and animal themes. In the beginning, therefore, decoration was abstract and the designs, like many-coloured fireworks, radiated in every direction from a central nucleus. The visitor admiring these fine vases may wonder how this ancient feeling of baroque came into being, and how in time it gave way to the forceful Greek geometric style. Yet this art, which is in the grip of an unrestrained fantasy and moves towards the unsymmetrical, rarely forgets that its function is to adorn the fragile surface of a vase; it always respects this basic fact, and remains, as one might say, intelligently decorative.

Floral and Marine style

The creative ceramic tradition continues into the following period, that of the new palaces (1700-1450 B.C.). Among the rich decorative elements of the Kamares style there gradually appear plant and animal forms which take the place of abstract designs, while in time the colour relation between decoration and surface is reversed: there is now dark decoration on a light-coloured ground. Large elegant vases have a flexible floral decoration: a "gentle and airy naturalism", a delicate exploitation of form, design and decorative composition gives grace and charm to these vases. Two styles, named "floral" and "marine" prevail, and are now typical of Minoan pottery. Stirrup-jars and flasks are most skilfully decorated with the form of the octopus that spreads its twining feelers and covers the whole surface of the vase (fig. 20). Rhyta of severe shape are decorated with the wealth of the sea, including the nautilus, the murex, the starfish and coral. At the same time every sort of plant form — lily, papyrus, crocus, iris, and foliage — seems to retain the freshness of the plant while giving the impression of a unique geometrical ornament (figs. 22-23).

Palace style

The infiltration of geometrical severity was accomplished in the last phase of the New Palace period. We cannot yet be certain whether this were the consequence of Mycenaean influence from the continent or the historical development of tendencies already existing in the previous two styles. The result, however, is striking, and the so-called "palace" style constitutes the remarkable last chapter to a long artistic chronicle. This last development was confined to Knossos: examples of this style were found only in the splendid palace of Knossos. The large vases with their severe construction and ornament, where wild plants and wild creatures of the sea begin to obey geometrical principles and architectural forms, have their own stately force. The lively Minoan impulse, the love of movement, the fascination of the curve are ever-present. These, however, are now subjected to a geometric stylization, and the acceptance of more rhythmical and rational principles indicates that a new spirit has breathed among them (fig. 24). Even if there had been no destruction by the forces of nature, Minoan art would have given place to another art, based on more forceful powers.

Stone-carving

Stone-carving is an art that particularly flourished at every stage of Minoan civilization. Even if the Cycladeans and the Egyptians gave the first lessons in stone work to the Minoan craftsmen — and this seems very probable — we can say that not only did the Minoans perfectly assimilate this foreign instruction, but that they very quickly outstripped their masters. Already from the Pre-Palace period stone vessels, which are real works of art, were being made in Crete. The stone chosen offered a wealth of colour and endless possibilities for the exploitation of its veining: many-coloured marble, steatite, basalt, alabaster were chiselled with admirable skill. Many unusual shapes were created, some of the greatest elegance, with their small handles, ingenious spouts, turned bases and curved lips. The veining was particularly well employed, to emphasize the shape of the vase, to bring out its articulation or to make its functional features distinct.

In the Old Palace period the splendour of the Kamares Ware somewhat eclipses the stone work. Nevertheless the production of stone vases continues, and their quality remains at a high level. The technical experience and the artistic sensibility of the early stone-cutters was to bequeath a rich heritage to the following and most flourishing period of Minoan civilization.

By this time craftsmen have learned how to work with more ease in the harder stones, basalt, porphyry, rock-crystal etc., and succeed in creating elaborate and dynamic shapes whose perfection gives form to the most daring fantasy, while the exploitation of the coloured veins in the stone shows remarkable intelligence and sensibility (fig. 25). The stone vessels from the treasuries of the sanctuaries of the palaces of Knossos and Zakros are among the most valuable collections of the Museum of Herakleion.

Stone vases with representations in relief

Among the ceremonial stone vessels of the New Palace period there is a category which deserves a special place not only in the history of Minoan stone-carving, but in that of Minoan art as a whole. A series of rhyta in black steatite have relief representations on their surface. Their significance is manifold; for the first time we have anthropomorphic representations depicting scenes from Cretan life; these representations, which exhibit surprising skill in execution and composition, confirm that the palace frescoes were not the only works in which human figures predominate in the artist's repertoire.

Scenes with many figures, like the festal procession of harvesters with their lively movements, on the rhyton from Hagia Triada, (figs. 28-29), and scenes of athletic life, with the incredibly daring stance of the athletes, on the other rhyton from Hagia Triada (fig. 26), show the same skill in design, in composition and in the plastic rendering of the human body as do the simpler but striking figures of the young warriors on the Chieftain Cup (again from Hagia Triada, fig. 27), and they are not at all inferior to the charming agricultural-religious composition of the wild goats climbing the rocks of the peak sanctuary on the rhyton of Zakros.

These able craftsmen sometimes gave the form of an animal to a whole stone vase: rhyta have the shape of a bull's head, whether carved in black steatite (palace of Knossos, fig. 32), or green chlorite (palace of Zakros), and a marble rhyton is in the shape of a lioness' head. These exquisite specimens are evidence of the artist's skill and talent and denote his fondness not only of the work but also of the animal depicted.

THE MINOR ARTS: Seal-engraving

In seal-engraving, a branch of art in which they were unique, the Minoan craftsmen showed their skill in impressing on hard stone, the most difficult of materials, the animal world in such a way as to exhibit both a perfect knowledge of that world and of the requirements of art. The making of seal-stones begins in the Pre-Palace period, at first in soft stone, and later in hard semi-precious stones. In the Old Palace period the seal-engravers worked in agate, sard, jasper, haematite, amethyst and other semi-precious stones, and with astonishing accuracy they succeeded in representing countless forms from the natural and animal world on the limited surfaces of the seals. But as in other branches of art, so also in seal-engraving, the New Palace period was the most creative. Not only is there a far greater quantity of seals, but their quality is incomparable; without exaggeration we may call them works of a great art. With the crystal purity of design, the cunning exploitation of space, and the admirably studied composition, the scenes represented on the small, bright-coloured surface of the stone give a unique aesthetic pleasure (fig.34): the life of nature, the violent conflicts between animals, religious scenes, bull-fights, birds and trees, men and monsters, all are living, and yet they are all subdued to the discipline demanded by this art of miniature, an art in which we find all the characteristics of Minoan civilization — the love for the artistic and the elegant, for liveliness and movement, for colour and light, but not for large dimensions and monumental effects.

Minor sculpture

The Cretans always remained faithful to their character and to their forms of artistic self-expression, and never attempted to imitate their neighbours — e.g. the Egyptians — in the creation of huge works of sculpture. We shall search in vain for works of major sculpture for, despite the fact that Minoan art with its knowledge of the human body early felt the need to give it plastic representation, it was always satisfied with figures of a small size, as the clay and bronze examples of the Old Palace period testify. In the New Palace period Minoan minor sculpture succeeded, by the use of precious and delicate material, in the production of unique masterpieces. The statuettes of the Snake Goddess in faience, with her rich and elegant Minoan robe, slender waist, characteristically protruding breasts and outstretched arms with the snakes, combine plastic feeling with love of colour, a permanent feature in Minoan art (figs. 18 and 38). Of an ivory composition that represented a bull-jumper on the horns of the bull, we have only the figure of the young athlete and even this is incomplete — the gold parts of the work are missing. This acrobat-athlete is shown at the moment when he has grasped the bull's horns with both his hands and with a vigorous motion of the feet backwards and upwards he is about to turn a somersault (fig. 30). The rendering of this unique moment, when all the limbs of the body have become tense as a spring, leaves us amazed at the artist's daring and at his almost incredible dexterity.

Work in gold

The Minoan goldsmiths also move with ease in this world of elegant miniature art. Since the Pre-Palace period they had already learned to make use of filigree and granulation. Bracelets and hair ornaments, necklaces and rings of delicate form, decorated with floral and animal motifs, are revealing of the wealth of Minoan society and its fondness of these elegant and charming objects (figs. 42-48). Throughout all the periods of Minoan civilization the creation of jewellery from gold and precious stones continued, with ever increasing artistic imagination and technical skill. It is enough to have seen the two wasps from Chrysolakkos at Malia sipping a drop of honey (fig. 47), to understand the perfect execution, the exquisite purity of the forms and the masterly combination of the parts that compose the whole. And even the zoomorphic beads representing lions, stags, wild goats etc., or others that represent miniature plants, flowers or fruits, not only exhibit the exterior form of the world of nature, but also its essence, in a rendering of it that, while subject to the principles of art, can preserve the vitality of living things.

Metal-work

In all creative periods art is not confined to the production of works, outside everyday life and its needs, but it permeates all human creations, even the most humble and useful. This can be observed in the Museum of Herakleion whose collections include household vessels and tools, as well as weapons and sacred axes. The metal-workers of the palaces, especially of the New Palace period, rivalled the other craftsmen both in their careful manufacture and in their handsome form and ornament. Some of the daggers and swords are true works of art: archaeologists doubt whether these had been actually used as weapons and believe that they merely formed part of the elegant ornaments worn by their noble and rich owners.

WALL-PAINTINGS

Having seen in a short general review all the creations of Minoan civilization, which enable us to imagine its wealth, artistic sensibility, and unique character, we may turn and admire one of the most striking examples of its art, the large paintings that covered the walls of great and small palaces, of rich villas and noble houses, bringing to life the places where men lived who rejoiced in this civilization (figs. 49-52). The surviving remains of these vast frescoes are scarce and their place in the whole composition is often uncertain; nevertheless there is enough to allow us to form an idea of the quality and essential characteristics of Minoan painting, which followed the same principles as the other arts and was the true expression of Minoan society. It did not adopt unassimilable loans from the other great contemporary civilizations, e.g. the Egyptian. In none of the Minoan frescoes do we find the representation of historical events or the apotheosis of kings, encountered in the monumental compositions of the great kingdoms of that time. In painting, as in the other arts, what dominates is the love of the natural world, and of social and religious life. However we do not find anywhere the "naturalism" which so many seem to have discerned. Forms and colours are subject to the laws of art, and subserve the decorative purpose of the frescoes. The artists are aware that the walls where they paint their conceptions are a solid element which they have no right to destroy; thus they create a kind of painting that expands in two dimensions, and never tries to attain an effect of depth. The same principles are behind the use of colour which spreads over the broad clear surfaces without aimless chromatic gradations and without any attempt at *trompe l'oeil* effects. Some historians who have studied Minoan art like to use the term "chromatic silhouette" as an accurate description of this deliberately flat painting that wisely ignores or denies the depth of the subject. The colour scale is exactly in keeping with this principle. Red and green, blue and yellow, beside black and white, the basic colours of the spectrum suffice, with a few touches of varied colour, to form a vivid and delightful harmony able to brighten the walls with mediterranean light, without making violent breaks in them. This chromatic tact is completed by the fine draughtsmanship of the forms: their clear design, their forceful but always delicate curved outline, their harmonious composition — like a musical unity — where every element contributes its clear tone to complete the harmony of the whole. The plants and beasts which earn their place in this harmony, have acquired their colour and shape from the requirements of fresco-painting, not from their counterparts in nature. For this reason it is often difficult and sometimes impossible to determine the kinds of plants or animals depicted.

Wall-paintings in low relief

In an early phase, soon after 1600 B.C., the Minoan artists, possibly under the influence of Egyptian models, created a type of composition in fresco which combines painting with low relief. The figures modelled in plaster are given an almost imperceptible inflation, which is nevertheless hidden under the vivid colouring. Such compositions include the famous "Prince with the Lilies" (in fact the Priest-King) (fig. 51), the remarkable bull from the north entrance to the palace of Knossos, and various "Ladies" from Eastern Crete. The fact that this device was not farther pursued shows the fidelity of the Cretan craftsmen to the principles of their art.

The large frescoes

The large compositions with many-figured scenes have particular significance for our knowledge of Minoan painting. Here we see the human form play a predominant role beside forms from the plant and animal world — as we have seen in the works of minor sculpture. There are religious scenes in which charming priestesses or goddesses (such as the celebrated "Parisienne", fig. 49) receive offerings or watch priestly ceremonies; processions where slender youths carry solemnly and gracefully elegant vases to the queen or goddess; and social gatherings, which Evans called "garden parties", where hundreds of miniature female figures are represented making lively gesticulations — they are evidently watching dances or contests from verandahs. There are also scenes showing such contests, for example the "bull-jumping", where the fearful strength of the bull and the elastic agility of the acrobat-athlete make a wonderful combination (fig. 52).

The sarcophagus of Hagia Triada

The unique stone sarcophagus found at Hagia Triada (fig. 53) is valuable from many points of view. It is unique in its rich painted decoration which depicts scenes of offerings, libations to the dead, chariots etc. Difficult as it is to interpret its religious symbolism, it excites the special interest of both the archaeologist and the layman, and is a remarkable example of the last years of Minoan painting; nevertheless it can at once be perceived that although its religious and archaeological interest is of particular significance, the artistic quality of the painting does not correspond to its archaeological value.

Sub-Minoan phase

After the end of Minoan civilization, c. 1100 B.C., and before the appearance of what we call Geometric art, Crete, like the rest of Greece, passed through a transitional period, here called the Sub-Minoan, insignificant from the point of view of civilization, since the once flourishing centres were ruined and only remote districts preserved agricultural settlements. The Minoans, however, retained their ancient beliefs, and thus the very ancient Minoan goddess with raised arms was worshipped in the sanctuaries of these settlements, as many idols in this form testify (figs. 54-55).

ARCHAIC GREEK ART

The splendour of Minoan art gives the Museum its special character. In the historical age, however, there was one more creative period, which though brief in duration and limited in extension, made Crete worthy to be distinguished among other Greek provinces. In the last years of the 8th and throughout the 7th century B.C. art in Crete made a robust and rich appearance. First ceramic and metal-work and then major sculpture produced so significant and original works that curiosity is excited about the historical causes for this renaissance and its sudden and swift end. In a small wing of the Herakleion Museum the visitor may see some of the most remarkable works of early Greek art — that which we call Archaic — from its first stage, the orientalizing, until the mature period when better examples are found in other areas.

It is worthy of note that some archaeologists call this ''orientalizing'' Greek art ''art of the Idaean style'', because they believe that its most typical examples, those which show beyond doubt the sources of influence, are the finds from the Idaean cave in Crete which are the first impressive exhibits in this part of the Museum: bronze shields with reliefs of the Great Goddess, the ''Lady of wild beasts'', with hunting scenes or representations of lions and griffins, and the great bronze *tympanon* which depicts the God who overcomes wild beasts. These works are so obviously oriental in origin that the only doubt that archaeologists can entertain is whether to attribute them to foreign artists established in Crete, or to Cretan artists who had studied in the East (fig. 57). There can be no doubt that Cretan craftsmen made the three statuettes of Apollo, Leto and Artemis: those hammered bronze figures found in the Archaic temple of Dreros, are the earliest and almost unique examples of this technique. To Cretan artists also are due the bronze sheets where a fine technique has rendered the human form so vividly.

Many have supported the hypothesis that Crete was the place where Greek major sculpture came into being, though all specialists have not been convinced of this. Nevertheless everyone agrees that the stone reliefs of Cretan work that belong to the second half of the 7th century B.C. testify to admirable technical accomplishment and unusual artistic vision (fig. 58). What survives in the Museum of Herakleion is only a small part of a rich and significant production, but it is sufficient to allow us to estimate accurately the contribution of this great island to the common endeavour of a most productive epoch, in which the strong foundations were laid of the whole superstructure that was to give glory to Greece in the following centuries. And it is a splendid prelude to the history of Greek art that we may follow in unbroken continuity in the other museums of modern Greece.

1. General view of the palace of Knossos (air photograph). The intricate architectural arrangements and refined luxury of this compound are typical of the New Palace period, at which time the palace reached its prime.

2. *A section of the north entrance to the palace of Knossos, with its restored turret, its relief mural of a bull and its great pillared hall. This entrance was connected with the road that led to the harbour.*

3. *View of the processional corridor leading from the south end of the palace of Knossos to the central court. The sacred double horns decorated an opening in the wall. In the foreground, large jars from the palace store-rooms.*

4

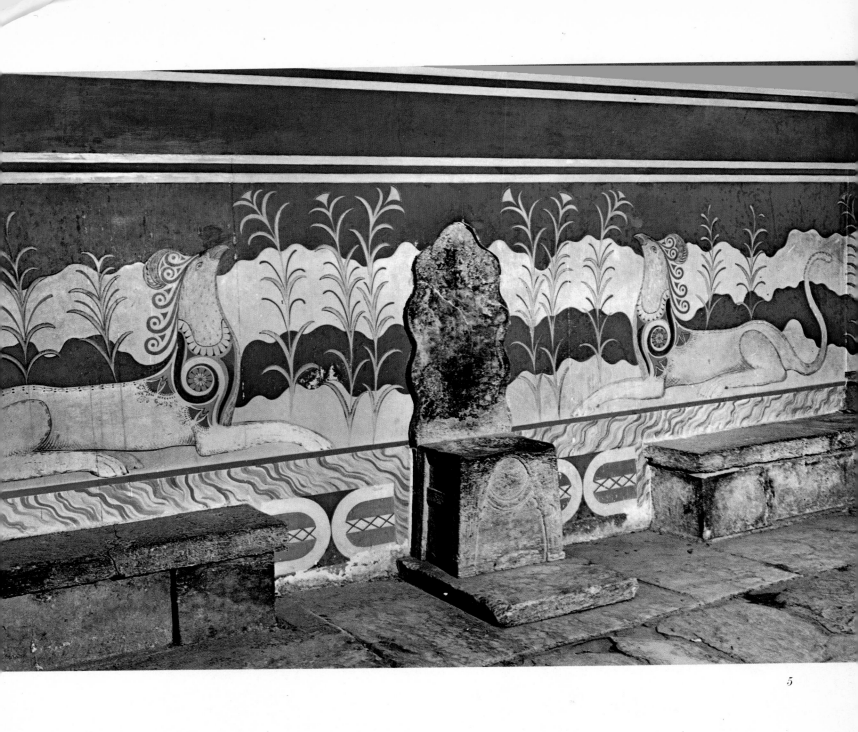

5

4. *Restored drawing of the west wing of the palace, as seen from the central court. In the middle of the two-storied façade, the sanctuary is crowned by a row of double horns. The staircase on the right leads to the second floor, which included the ceremonial chambers.*

5. *The room of the sacred throne constituted the main part of the sanctuary in the west wing. The throne—which was the seat of the Priest-King—was flanked by sacred griffins painted on the wall. Seats for the priests lined the walls on either side.*

6

7

6. *The palace of Phaistos was built on a low hill west of the Mesara plain. The air photograph shows a large part of the palace complex, including the west court and the theatral area.*

7. *View of the stepped theatral area and the retaining wall of the north court at the palace of Phaistos.*

8. *The palace of Malia, of lesser importance than that of Knossos and Phaistos, stood at the centre of a fairly extensive urban quarter. The architectural arrangement (multi-storied wings, staircases, store-rooms) around the central courtyard is typical of Minoan palaces. (Air photograph.)*

9. *The royal road at the palace of Malia, leading to the north entrance. The two Old Palace pithoi (jars) shown in the photograph were found in the store-rooms.*

10. *Circular kernos (stone dish for miscellaneous offerings) from the palace of Malia. It was used as a ceremonial table of offerings where the faithful placed small quantities of corn, pulse, oil, etc. from their crops.*

8

9

10

11

12

11. *View of the bay of Kato Zakros, with the palace in the centre. Its position at the east end of the island of Crete facilitated close trade contacts with Egypt and the East. (Air photograph.)*

12. *The archaeological site of Tylissos. The surviving ruins belong to the villas of local noblemen. (Air photograph.)*

13. North view of the large villa of Hagia Triada. It was probably the summer residence of the princes of Phaistos. (Air photograph.)

14. The villa of Hagia Triada seen from the west. The photograph shows the two wings arranged at an angle on either side of the central courtyard. (Air photograph.)

14

15. *Farm-house of a local Minoan nobleman at Bathypetro in central Crete. The various farming installations (wine-press, oil-press) and the handicraft workshops discovered on this site are of special importance.*

16. *The cave of Eileithyia at Amnisos, the port of Knossos. The two stalagmites visible in the photograph were initially thought to have been idols of the Mother-goddess and child; the faithful had built around them a low wall, upon which they placed their offerings.*

17

17. Ruins of a villa at Amnisos. The lily-frescoes discovered here are kept in the Museum. According to ancient texts, king Minos used Amnisos as his port.

18. The smaller 'Snake Goddess'. Faience statuette found in the 'central sanctuary' crypt of the Palace of Knossos. 1600-1580 B.C.

19. *Fruit bowl from Phaistos in the Kamares style. Particularly admirable is the spiral design on the inside of the bowl. c. 1800 B.C.*

20. *Nine-handled vase. Decorated with octopuses beautifully twining their tentacles over the surface of the vase. A brilliant example of the Marine style. c. 1450 B.C.*

21. *Krater with sculptured decoration of flowers. A 'baroque' creation in the Kamares style from the Old Palace of Phaistos. c. 1800 B.C.*

22. *Beak-spouted jug, decorated with dense foliage which gives the impression of a geometric ornament. A characteristic example of the Floral style. c. 1530-1500 B.C.*

19

20

21

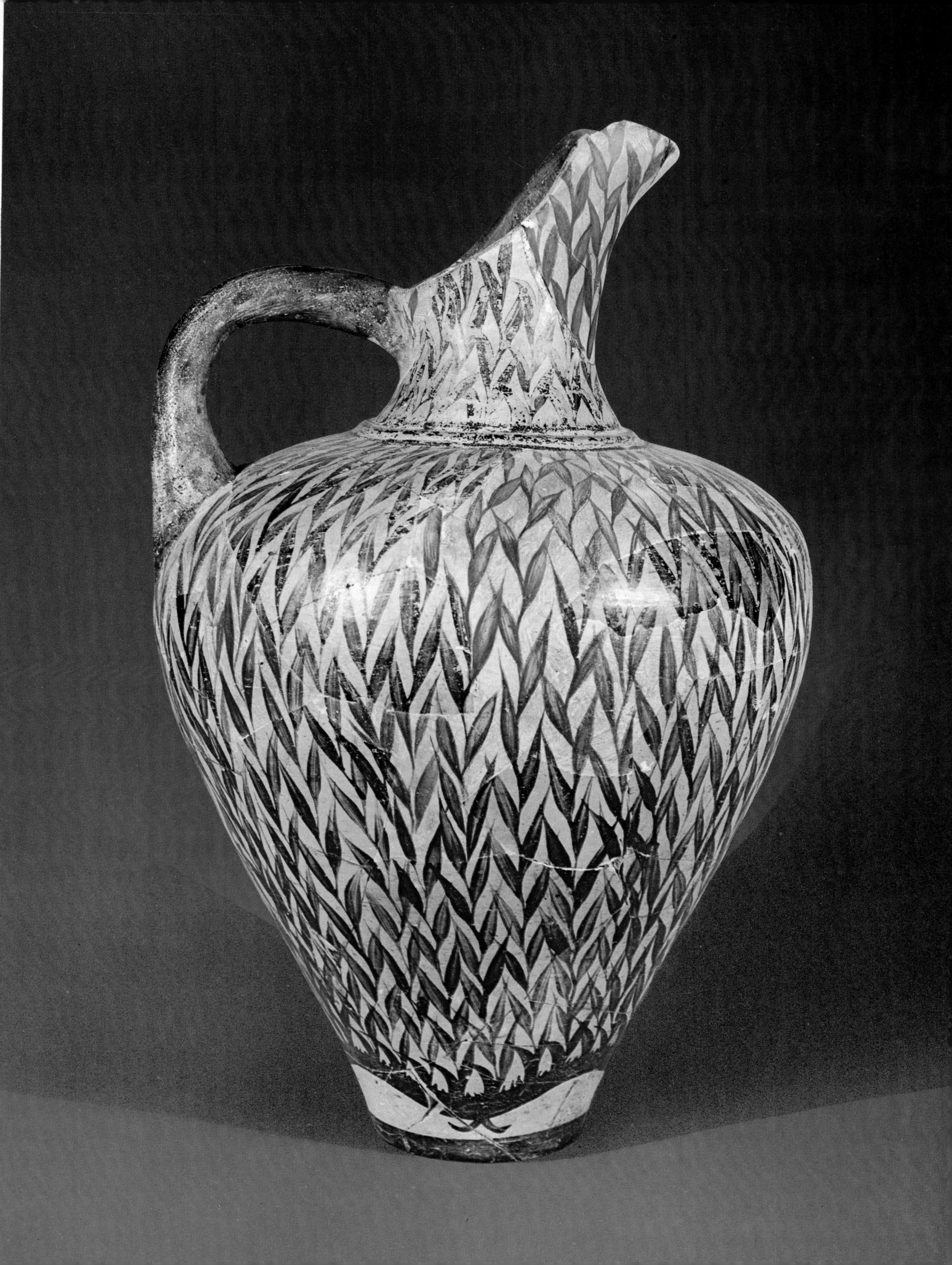

23. *Rhyton decorated with starfish and shells. A characteristic example of the Marine style. c. 1500 B.C.*

24. *Libation jug with beak-shaped spout and very delicate neck, exceptionally elaborate both in shape and decoration. An example of the last years of the New Palace period. c. 1400 B.C.*

25. *Beautiful ceremonial vase from the 'basin of purification' at Zakros. Unique in the skilful and clever use of coloured marble and in the astonishing sensitivity and boldness of its shape. c. 1450 B.C.*

23

24

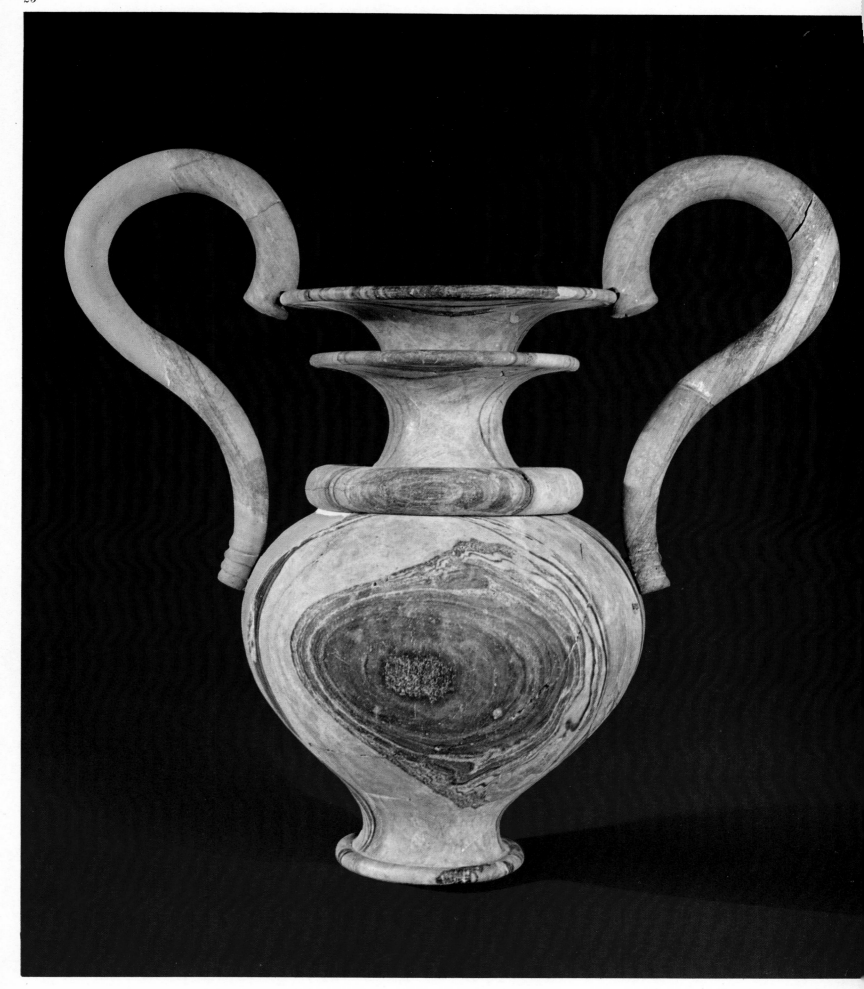

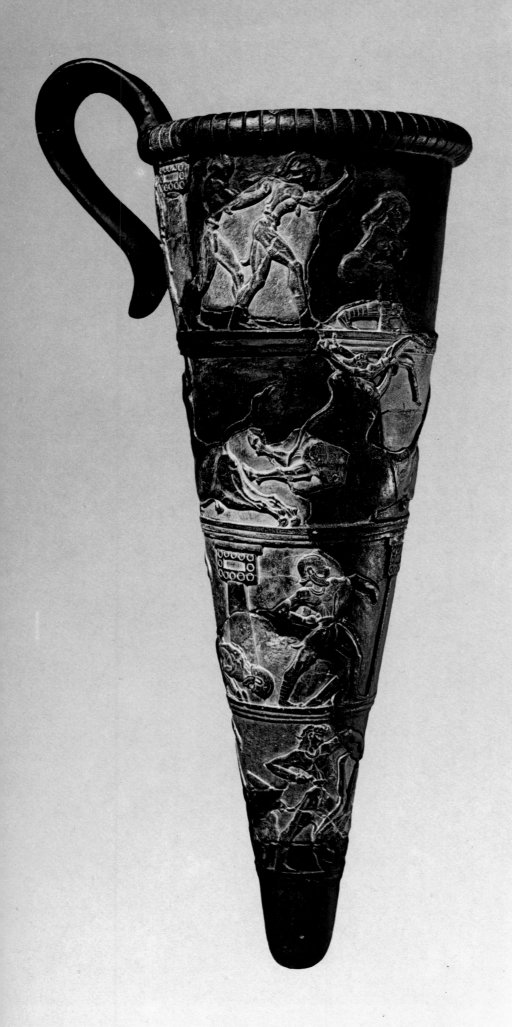

26. Steatite rhyton with representations in relief divided into four zones: top zone, wrestling; second zone, bull-jumping; next, helmeted men boxing; and bottom zone, young men boxing. Found at Hagia Triada. 1550-1500 B.C.

27. Steatite vase with representations in relief, known as 'the Prince's Drinking-Cup'. An imposing figure, sceptre in hand, stands in front of a building; turned towards him, is a young man with helmet, sword and a tasseled wand; behind him are three men carrying the skins of large animals. Found at Hagia Triada. 1550-1500 B.C.

28-29. The famous 'Harvester Vase' from Hagia Triada, a masterpiece of Minoan stone-carving. The representation shows a group of men, returning from farm work carrying their tools on their shoulders; the procession is headed by singing musicians; the first musician carries a seistron. 1550-1500 B.C.

26

27

28

29

30

30. The 'Bull-Jumper'. Ivory figure of an athlete at the moment of turning a somersault over the horns of the bull (which has not been preserved). c. 1550 B.C.

31. Head of a royal sceptre made of schist stone. The handle is in the shape of a leopard at one end and that of an axe at the other. Palace of Malia. c. 1650 B.C.

32. A superb steatite rhyton in the shape of a bull's head. The horns (now lost) were made of gilded wood, the eye of rock-crystal, and the white around the nostril of shell. Little Palace of Knossos. 1550-1500 B.C.

31

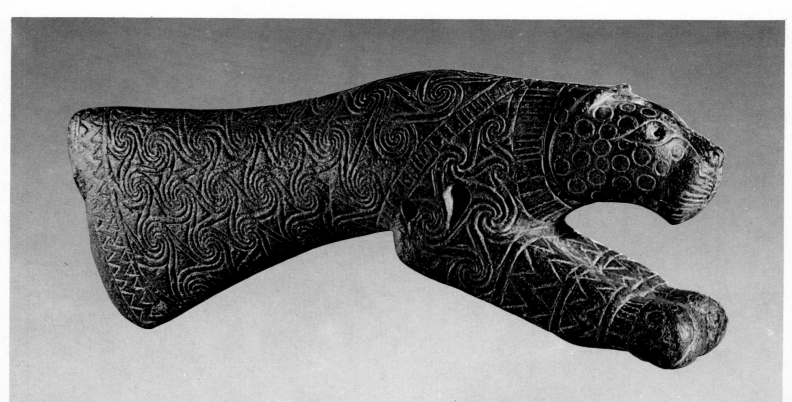

33. *An exquisite rock-crystal rhyton. The crystal ring at the neck is decorated with gilt faience; the beads on the handle were wound together with bronze wire. Palace of Zakros. c. 1450 B.C.*

34. *The seal-engraving art of the New Palace period in Minoan Crete created real masterpieces: the miniature figures engraved with great accuracy on hard semi-precious stones have both plastic completeness and incomparable expressive forcefulness.*
a) haematite seal-stone: lioness attacking a bull; b) sard seal-stone: fine representation of bulls; c) chalcedony seal-stone set in gold: lion and tamers; d) cyanos seal-stone set in gold: lion and male figure (god?); e) sardonyx seal-stone: goddess between winged griffins, the double axe over her head.

34

b

d

35

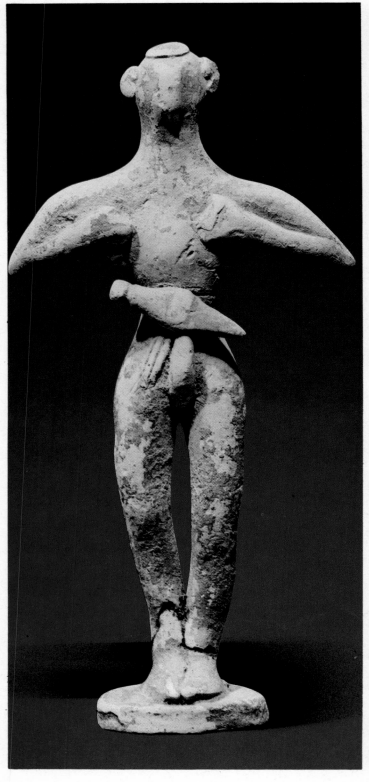

36

37

35. Clay statuette from the 'Peak sanctuary' of Petsofa. It represents a worshipper, as is indicated by the position of his hands on his breast; he wears a belt with a dagger. c. 1950 B.C.

36-37. Faience plaques found in the repositories of the Palace of Knossos. The first represents a wild goat nursing her young. The second, a cow with her calf. The perfect feeling for natural forms, which is a major element of Minoan art, finds its most forceful expression in works of this kind. c. 1600 B.C.

38. The larger 'Snake Goddess', a faience statuette. A snake curls around her outstretched arms and body, its head reaching her tall headdress; she wears a long robe and an apron and her two breasts, symbols of fertility, are bare and characteristically protruding. c. 1600 B.C.

39

40

41

39. Faience plaques representing Minoan houses; they may have formed the decoration of a wooden chest and they depicted a whole town. In spite of their small size, they give us a clear picture of the multi-storied Minoan houses. 1700 - 1600 B.C.

40. The famous 'Disk of Phaistos'. Hieroglyphic symbols, each an independent character, are imprinted in the circular clay disk, on both sides. Archaeologists have not succeeded in deciphering the script, and its content remains unknown. It is presumed to be a hymn to a divinity. c. 1600 B.C.

41. Bronze statuette from Tylissos. It represents a young man wearing the Minoan loin-cloth; he has a necklace and bracelets on his wrists and ankles. His right arm is lifted to his forehead in the characteristic position of salutation or prayer to a divinity, while his left arm is stretched out and resting on his thigh. c. 1500 B.C.

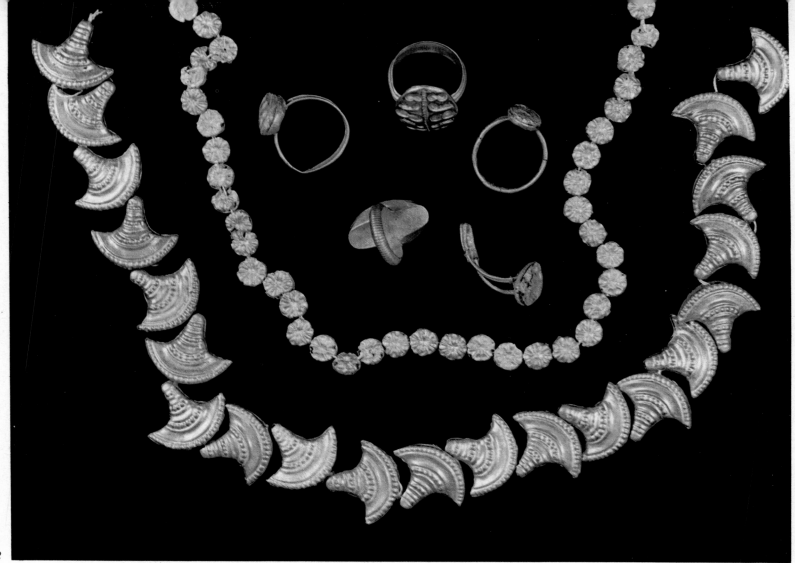

42

43

42. Gold jewellery from the region of Archanes. c. 1400 B.C.

43. Gold Minoan objects. The double axes come from the sanctuary in the cave of Arkalochori. Before 1600 B.C. The other two objects are earrings and come from Mavro Spelio near Knossos. c. 1450 B.C.

44   45   46

44. Gold necklace bead in the shape of a lion, from Hagia Triada. c. 1500 B.C.

45. Gold pendant in the shape of a bull's head, from Zakros. c. 1450 B.C.

46. Gold necklace bead in the shape of a duck, from the Palace of Knossos. c. 1500 B.C.

47. Gold ornament, accessory to a necklace, from Chryssolakkos at Malia. Two wasps are sipping a drop of honey. An exquisite example of Minoan gold-work. c. 1500 B.C.

48. Gold ring from a tomb at Isopata, decorated with a cult scene. Four female figures with long Minoan robes and bare breasts stand in a floral landscape. Many believe this scene to represent an 'epiphany' of the goddess. c. 1500 B.C.

47   48

49. *The celebrated 'Parisienne' of the Palace of Knossos. It is a fragment from the fresco of 'libation offerings', as it has been named by the archaeologists, who believe that this figure represents a priestess. c. 1500-1450 B.C.*

50. *Fragment from a larger fresco found in the 'House of frescoes' at Knossos. It represents a bird, named the 'Blue Bird' because of its colour. The rest of the fresco might have represented royal gardens with exotic birds. c. 1500 B.C.*

51. *Colour relief of the 'Prince with the Lilies' or the 'Priest-King', as he has been called by experts. The slender young figure is wearing the Minoan loin-cloth and a splendid crown of lilies and peacock feathers. With his left hand, he was probably holding and leading a sacred animal, a sphinx or a griffin. Palace of Knossos. c. 1500 B.C.*

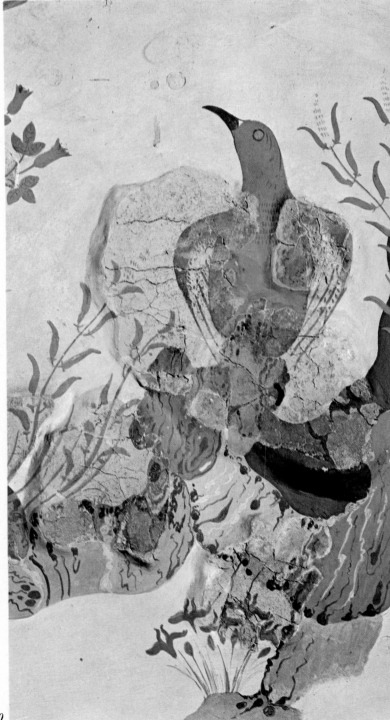

50